WHEN *Prophecies* *Fail*

A PRACTICAL RESPONSE TO THE
Voice *of* God

KIRBY CLEMENTS SR.

CLEMENTS
MINISTRIES

Decatur, Georgia

When Prophecies Fail
Copyright 2017 Kirby Clements Sr.

Address inquiries to the publisher:

Clements Ministries
2000 Cathedral Place
Decatur, Georgia 30034 USA

Learn more about the author at
www.clementsministries.org

ISBN: 978-0-9968702-1-4 (print)
ISBN: 978-0-9968702-2-1 (ebook)

Library of Congress Control Number: 2017961451

First Printing: June 1999
Second Printing: December 2017

Printed in the United States of America

ACKNOWLEDGMENTS

Our gratitude and thanks to the following people who gave of their time and skills:

Janette Donaldson
Charlotte Lemons

FOREWORD

Here is a book that gives some vital insight concerning why some prophecies fail to come to pass.

Dr. Kirby Clements is a man of great integrity and honesty. He loves truth and the practice of it with biblical wisdom. For the deep thinkers and seekers of truth, this book will be a great blessing.

Dr. Kirby covers the root problem of prophecies concerning the end times. Our theological concepts affect how we interpret prophetic scriptures concerning the destiny of the Church, planet earth and the Kingdom of God.

In the section dealing with prophecies to individuals and coming events key principles are given to determine why some prophecies fail. This book is not designed to be an exhaustive study on the subject of prophecy but enough truth and challenging thoughts are given to put the reader on the path of right attitudes and actions to be taken concerning prophecy and its fulfillment. Guidelines are given concerning what causes prophecies to fail.

This book is a must for those who want to fulfill every prophecy they have received and know what to do "When Prophecies Fail." I highly recommend this book to every Christian and I fully endorse the character and wisdom of the author. One truth that will help us conform to the image of Christ and fulfill our prophetic destiny is more valuable than a million dollars. You will receive at least a million dollars worth of value from this book.

Dr. Bill Hamon
Bishop/Founder/President of Christian
International Ministries Network

INTRODUCTION

Christianity is a propositional, experiential and representative faith. It is a propositional faith because there are series of conditions that require an attitudinal and behavioral response. For example, anyone that comes to God must first believe that He is God and that He is a rewarder of those who diligently seek Him; and if anyone believe in their heart and confess with their mouth, the Lord Jesus, they shall be saved. Christianity is an experiential faith since the redemptive process involves a relationship with the Lord. Jesus declared the conditions of such a relationship when he said: "If a man loves me, he will keep my word; and my Father will love him, and we will come unto him, and make our abode with him" (John 14:23). Humanity experiences divinity and divinity experienced being human. Christianity is a representative faith because

as Christians we are called to take that,
which we have seen, heard, and handled of
the Word of life and declare it unto others.
Jesus' commandment to the disciples and to
us all was to go into all the world and make
disciples of all people (Matt. 28:19). Jesus
represented mankind in the atonement and
redeemed humanity represents God's cause
on earth. Redemption is therefore propositional, experiential and representative.

Christianity is also subjective and objective. The objective aspect of the faith is
supposed to involve the use of facts without
distortion by personal feelings or prejudic-
es. The objectivity of the faith should involve a minimizing of the personal creative
interpretation and relates to Peter's word
that "no prophecy of scripture is of a private interpretation" (2 Peter 1:20). Objectivity demands that some universal beliefs
and conclusions are repeatable or that different believers, independent of one anoth-

er, have adopted the same creeds or doctrines. It is referred to as orthodoxy and perhaps should involve some repeatable principles of interpretation, which ultimately reach the same conclusions. In most circles this is referred to as hermeneutics However, even the basis of what should be a source of an objective aspect of the faith is often fragmented into different school of thought. The subjective aspect of Christianity involves the personal and unique experiences of each individual. Because the subjective aspect often lacks verifiable proof and is related to experiences that cannot always be repeatable by different individuals, even under the same conditions, it is often questioned. Who can prove or disprove that the individual has experienced vision, a dream, an impression or a spiritual encounter? The correctness of the product of the experience may be measured by its alignment with established truths and facts but no one, except the individual, can verify the experience. So the Apostle Peter answers the scoffers who questioned the experiences of the apostles that they "Have not followed cunningly devised fables, when we made known unto you the power and coming of our Lord Jesus Christ, but were eyewitnesses of his majesty" (2 Peter 1:16).

It is the subjective aspect of faith that is often demonstrated in prophetic ministry that is to be addressed here. Prophecy is a communication tool of the Holy Spirit, with historical roots, and all true prophecy is a blending of the natural and the supernatural (Isaiah 14; Ezek. 28). It represents a convergence of the activities of the divine and the human (2 Peter 1:21). The messages of the prophets were predictive, corrective and instructive while expressing divine interests and exposing human behavior. The prophets served as divine prosecuting attorneys as they exposed violations of the law, revealed ordinances, and vindicated divine rights and privileges (Jer. 2:9,15:1-9; 25:31; Hosea 4:1). They also gave hope, promises of blessing and future destiny if God's people would obey (Isaiah 1:18; Jer. 29:11). And because the source of their messages was derived through a process of inspiration rather than the product of a written text, their contemporaries would often question the validity of their words (Jer. 28).

This process of prophetic activity has not ceased and still finds a significant place in the Christian faith today. Prophecy is still a vehicle of edification, exhortation, and comfort that reveals God's purposes and intentions. Its focus may involve a variety of interests ranging from politics, economics, world wars, and global weather events to end time matters.

In recent years, there has been an emphasis upon prophecy as it relates to the individual and to eschatology, the study of the final things. The predictive element of prophecy is of interest here, for it is quite obvious by now that much of the predictions concerning annihilation of the planet and the radical disruption of human life have fallen short. Many individuals are still living in the wake of unfulfilled personal prophecies. In this work, we shall endeavor to explore some of the causes and consequences of failed prophecies.

CONTENTS

PART ONE

Eschatological

Representing Deity

If we accept the Scriptures as the inspired historical record of divine interaction in human affairs, we are immediately faced with the question of how this interaction occurs and through what channels is this interaction mediated? Such words as visitations, visions, dreams, revelations and prophecies detail some of the channels of divine encounters. Prophets, kings, holy men and women experienced divine communications. Those individuals were often commissioned to communicate what they had seen and heard. The accuracy of that communication or representation has often been posed as an issue of interpretation.

Was the channel of transmission undiluted with human opinions? Was the process of inspiration a dictation event that was so imprinted upon the mind and spirit of the individual that very little opportunity was left for error? Was the process of being "moved upon by the Spirit" of such a nature that human faculties were so suspended as to facilitate a perfect transmission? Was the "hearer" or the "seer" left to interpret or translate the divine communication through the context of human personality and environmental conditioning? All of these questions have sparked debates and controversies in various theological circles. Regardless of the conclusions that have been reached, the fact of faith, personal experiences, and numerous confirmations from "sundry times and divers places" have convinced the author that divine interaction in human affairs is both a historical fact and a present truth. There is communication between heaven and earth.

The representative character of the Christian experience is of concern here. How do we "represent" God in our world? How do we serve *as a* symbol of God in our world? Beginning with Adam and Eve who were vice-regents of divine authority and continuing down through Moses, Abraham, Isaac, Jacob, Peter, James, John, Paul and the host of apostles and prophets, we had a parade of messengers who represented heavenly interests. They were far from being perfect specimens of righteous conduct and behavior. It was said of one of the prophets, Elias, that he was "a man subject to like passions as we are" (James 5:17). Paul presents his own defense before King Agrippa with the insistence that he was "not disobedient unto the heavenly vision" (Acts 26:19). How can imperfect humanity demonstrate the perfect and the infallible divinity? After all, we are encouraged by the Scriptures to "let our light so shine before men that they may see our good works, and glorify our Father which is in heaven" (Matt. 5:16). Once again, it is Pauline theology that proposes the convergence of the human and the divine in the formation of what is called a "new creature," and a "temple not made with hands" (Acts 17:24; 1 Cor. 3:16, 6:19; 2 Cor. 5:17-20). So if the individual believer, as part of the corporate body of believers called "the church" is to represent the source and agent of redemption, it will probably be through the proclamation and demonstration of the consequences of this divine encounter. It is the proclamation of a heavenly message that we wish to examine here.

God Hath Spoken, but What Did He Say?

The fact that God has spoken in history and continues to speak today is the source and evidence of our Christian faith. Godliness means hearing the word. Hearing is more than listening to what is spoken. To "hear" in the biblical sense, implies attention, assent, and application to oneself of the things learned; it means listening with a firm purpose to obey, and then doing *as* God's Word proves to require.[1] If the "Word of God" becomes the source of our beliefs and convictions, then there is a potential crisis that occurs during the moments of hearing the Word. That is, God has spoken but

what did He say? The crisis is one of interpretation. The Serpent posed the critical
question to Eve in the Garden when he
asked, "Hath God said?" (Gen. 3:1). And
since that moment, the interpretation of the
Word of God has been in part, the cause of
debates and has even been implicated as the
catalyst of many religious divisions called
denominations.[2] The different schools of
interpretation of the Old Testament prophets, the Psalms, the parables and the teachings of Jesus and the apostles have provided
ample opportunities for a variety of meanings. Jesus set the stage for the interpretative
process when he used parables to teach spiritual truths.[3] The messages of the prophets,
which touched upon the past, present and
future have been given literal and symbolical meanings. Much of the interpretations
of these vital scriptural narratives have
served as the basis for our Christian convictions and also for our divisions.

Prophecy is not simply limited to fore-telling. It may embrace foretelling of God's Word and may relate to the past, present and future. And the fulfillment of both the foretelling and foretelling ingredients of prophecy may come to pass in a surprising and unexpected manner. For example, the Jewish idea of the kingdom of God was fashioned by the interpretation of Old Testament prophecies concerning the age to come. The prophets spoke of the age of plenty (Amos 9:13,14; Isaiah 35:1,7, 51:3; Jer. 31:12), an age of peace (Isaiah 2:4, 11:6-9, 32:18, 65:25), the end of pain (Isaiah 33:24, 25:8, 65:20, 22) and a time when Jerusalem would be the center of the world (Isaiah 2:2, 45:14, 49:6, 60:12; Micah 4:1,2; Zech. 14:17,18). The vast majority of the Jews dreamed that in the days to come the Jewish nation would become master and ruler of all the world. They viewed themselves as God's chosen people;

therefore, some day God would exalt them above all other nations. As a chosen people, they viewed themselves as possessing special privileges rather than a people chosen for a special responsibility.[4] Israel thought that all the other nations existed to serve them, while God had intended that they should exist to serve all other nations.[5] The true meaning of "a royal priesthood" and "a holy nation" entailed the responsibility of representing divine authority before all nations with the intent of reconciling nations unto God. Therefore, the anticipated fulfillment of the Old Testament prophecies came to pass in a most surprising and unexpected manner.

E.W. Rogers in *Concerning the Future,* states that prophecy should be interpreted literally unless such literal interpretation is manifestly impossible because of the absurdity, in which case the underlying principle should be regarded as the chief

thing.[6] Rogers states that metaphors, fig-
ures of speech, and similes should be care-
fully distinguished from that which is literal, and where the literal yields good sense
it must not be assumed that the passage is
symbolic. Gary DeMar expresses the opin-
ion that the entire thesis of futurism rests
on a non-literal reading of the prophetic
texts.[7] Marvin Rosenthal expresses the idea
that this arbitrary manner of dealing with
Scripture has proven to be the foundation
of sand for the entire prophetic system
called dispensationalism and the newly
promoted pre-wrath rapture position.[8] Of
course, the opposite end of the interpretative spectrum is to disregard the "spiritual
dimension" of Scripture and to negate the
necessity of the Holy Spirit in the entire
process.

Prophecy, as a revelational tool, is
progressive and the various parts of the
prophetic word are of a homogeneous

whole and are mutually interdependent. Therefore, no prophecy is of its own independent interpretation, and earlier prophecies should govern the interpretation of subsequent prophecies. This progressive nature is seen in the promise made to Abram, "In thy seed all nations of the earth shall be blessed" (Gen. 12:3, 18:18), but subsequent prophecies indicated that not only the natural seed but also the spiritual seed was to become the channel of that blessing. It is also to be seen that "the nations of the earth" included Gentiles also. The early commission of the Lord Jesus to the disciples was to go only unto the house of Israel while the latter commission was to include all of the world.

The progressive nature of prophetic revelation (a coined phrase that relates to predictions and expectations) can be seen in *a* comparison between the book of Acts and the epistles. The early speeches in Acts do not reveal any expectation of a speedy return of the end of the age while the epistles show that such an expectation came to occupy a prominent place (2 Thes 1:7-8). Paul began his epistles with such a note of expectancy but he adjusted his view. If we consider the chronological order of his epistles we discover such a progression. In Romans there is the expectation that the final consummation will not occur until the Jews, as a body, turn to Christ (1:10). While in the later epistle to the Ephesians Paul does not focus upon the role of the Jews in the future. He instead reveals a process of reconciliation through Christ where the barrier between Jew and Gentile is broken down and the Church becomes the vehicle of salvation. There is no mention of the Second Advent for Paul expresses the significant benefits of the first coming of Christ. So progression of prophetic revelation involves a gradual unfolding of divine intentions and purposes while also witnessing a clearer understanding by the recipients.

Convictions, Behaviors
and Predictions

So there is a significant question to be posed: Does it matter what we believe? The answer may be obvious since the flames of convictions have fueled every religious, political or social movement. The English Revolution of the mid-seventeenth century, culminating in the great achievements of religious toleration a constitutional monarchy, was a product of many forces; the deepest and most powerful of these was religion—a personal religion, notably among the common people based on a study of the Bible and of the many works of devotion that poured from the presses in the 60 years up to 1640.[9] It was Martin Luther's belief in justification by faith that drove him to attack not simply the abuses of medieval Catholicism, but Catholicism itself as an abuse of the Gospel.[10] It was a modern day prophet with a similar name, Martin Luther King, Jr., whose belief in the redemptive value of undeserved suffering became the basis for the strategy of non-violence which highlighted the entire civil rights movement.[11] All reformative and revolutionary movements have been undergirded by strong convictions. Without convictions there are very few sustained revolutionary or reformation movements that come into existence whether they be social, political, religious or even personal.

Convictions are beliefs that demand strong behavioral commitments. Commitments may range from making public declarations to the neglect of personal concerns and the disposal of worldly goods.

When the convictions are of a religious nature they are at times organized around predictions or expectations concerning some future events or some moment in time. Many movements specify a time or period during which such predicted events will occur. Historically, many of these convictions have often centered around the second coming of Christ and the beginning of Christ's reign over the world; the disruption of life on this planet; or some cataclysmic event that will border on the annihilation of the planet with the anticipated rescue of some specific group of believers.

History has recorded an unusual combination of behavioral commitments precipitated by such strong convictions. Since the Apostolic days, many Christians have lived with the expectations of the imminent return of Christ. There is some general agreement among historians that me apostles were both convinced and committed to such a belief following the resurrection and the ascension.[12] When the event did not occur during the first century, one of the writers of the New Testament recorded that "one day with the Lord is as a thousand years" (2 Peter 3:8). However, rather than being disappointed over such a hope, the early Christians came to appreciate a reality they had already known: Christ had come; God's victory had been accomplished; and the new creation was already a realized fact. So they made the adjustment in the tension between realization and expectation in their theology and in their thinking and moved forward with greater confidence.

As the years turned into decades and centuries, it became obvious that the expected millennium had not been initiated with the resurrection of Jesus. Perhaps the Second Coming would be the initiating event. Justin Martyr (c.100-c.165), in his

Dialogue with Trypho, linked the beginning of the millennium with Christ's "Second Advent." Justin believed that there would be a resurrection of the faithful to live with Christ in the New Jerusalem. Once the millennium was completed, the balance of humanity would be resurrected and all would receive the Last Judgment. The writing of Justin seemed to be the first post-apostolic writing that connected the millennium with a period following the second coming. Perhaps Justin may have been the first premillennialist.

In the second century, Montanus predicted the coming of the Lord with the New Jerusalem descending from heaven to Pepuza in Asia Minor.[13] He based the authority of his predictions upon a personal "revelation" and his "prophetic predictions' influenced people to gather in such numbers that a new town sprang up to house them. When the predictions proved to be false the committed followers did not totally disband in despair; instead, the disconformation generated a fresh zeal among those who had committed themselves to uprooting their lives and relocating to a new town.[14]

In the early 200s, Hippolytus of Rome became one of the few early writers to predict the date of the Second Coming of Christ and the establishing of the millennium in 496.[15] Hippolytus told of a foolish Syrian church leader who had led his people into the desert to await the Second Coming.[16] When the disconfirmation came, the people were devastated and many questioned the Scriptures and even their faith.

Frank Rutter, in his work, *The Poetry of Architecture* maintains that during the ninth and tenth century very little construction of importance occurred in Italy or in Eastern Europe due to the expectation of the impending Day of Judgment.[17] However, a work by C.J. Hefele, *Histoire des Conciles,* denies that there existed such a wide spread belief in the imminent end of the age at the close of the tenth century which encouraged such a broad abandonment of construction.[18]

The Anabaptists of the early sixteenth century believed in the occurrence of a millennium in 1533.[19] The location of the New Jerusalem was determined, the true Gospel would now be preached throughout the earth, and the end of all things was at hand. As was the case with most millennial movements, the commitment and devotion of people was expressed in a disruption of their lives and an abandonment of all worldly pleasures.[20] When the predictions proved to be false the groups seemed to be fortified with new enthusiasm rather than being discomforted by the disconformation.

In the mid-nineteenth century, William Miller (1782-1849), a New England farmer, with a belief in the literal fulfillment of prophecy, predicted that the world would end in 1843.[21] He took the 2,300 days of Daniel 8:14 to mean so many years; and by taking the year 457 B.C. as his starting point he reached 1843 as the date of the Second Advent of Christ. The fact that Miller had specified a particular time for the coming of the Lord accounted for a tremendous amount of interest and enthusiasm among committed people. The followers of Miller took celestial signs such as the meteor shower of 1833 and the 1843 appearance of a huge comet, visible to the naked eye even in the daylight, as evidence of the truth of the preacher's prediction. A movement developed with its share of conferences, publications, and associations. Many left their business and, dressed in white muslin robes, they awaited the event on housetops and hills. When the discomformation did occur, the severe disappointment among the committed believers was only brief before a new energy and zeal was awakened.[22] Later they divided into four sects, with the larger proportion forming the Seventh-day Adventists.

By 1875 dispensationalism began to flourish in the United States following its success in Britain among the Plymouth Brethren. It was C.I. Scofield (1843-1921), who popularized the system of premillennialism and the secret, any-moment, pre-tribulational rapture ("catching away") of the church that was developed by John Nelson Darby. The premillennialists focused upon current problems of society and interpreted them as "signs of the times." Worldliness in the church, political corruption, wars, international conflicts, liberal theology, earthquakes, forest fires, epidemics, changing weather patterns, the rise of Zionism, the sinking of the Titanic, the partitioning of Europe after World War I, the rise of religious cults, the desecration of the Lord's Day by immigrants and even radio were taken as countless events and trends that pointed to the end of the age. This movement with its scores of Bible institutes founded between 1880 and 1940, was responsible for the orientations of pastors, evangelists, Bible teachers, missionaries, youth workers and many others in the concept of premillennialism.

Premillennialism escalated following the end of World War II. The advent of atomic weapons provided an atmosphere for fear and the threat of thermonuclear annihilation. The Cold War between the United States and the Soviet Union was portrayed as an ideological battle rather than a geopolitical conflict. This controversy between capitalism and communism provided the fire for a lot of the prophetic and apocalyptic literature that was produced in the 1960s through the 1980s. With the creation of the Jewish State of Israel in 1948, the recovery of Jerusalem in 1967, the rise of Russia, the European integration, military power in East Asia, an Arab confederation organized against Israel, the rise of occultism, the apostasy of the Christian churches, the movement toward a one-world government, and the decline of the United States as a world power, the stage was set for an "Armageddon" battle. According to premillennial theory, Christ will suddenly appear just as the battle ensues and He will deliver believers from the impending destruction. It was predicted that Christ would return in 1988 and the rapture of the church would occur in 1995.

Throughout the history of the Watchtower Bible and Tract Society, many leaders have given predictions concerning the end time. In 1914, Charles Taze Russell, founder of the Watchtower Bible and Tract Society, declared that the final end of the kingdoms of this world was at hand and that the establishment of the kingdom of God would be achieved at the end of 1914.[23]

Herbert W. Armstrong, founder of the Worldwide Church of God, predicted a famine and disease epidemic that would affect one third of the entire population. Armstrong wrote, "this drought will be even more devastating than he foresees, and that it will strike sooner than 1975, probably between 1965 and 1972! This will be the very beginning, as Jesus said, of the Great Tribulation!"[24]

Richard Abanes lists many of the other end-time predictions that have been given over the centuries including those of Christopher Columbus (1556), the Shakers (1792), Jehovah's Witness (1914), Charles Taylor (1976, 1980, 1981-1989, 1992 and

1994), Hal Lindsey (1981), Lester Sumrall (1985), Louis Farrakhan (1991) and others.[25]

A religious sect in Kanungu, Uganda predicted the world would end on December 31, 1999.[26] Members of the Movement for the Restoration of the Ten Commandments of God surrendered all their belongings and prepared to go to another world. The unfulfilled prophecy of the sect cost the faith and the lives of many loyal followers. The failure of the prediction led members to demand belongings they had surrendered to the religious sect. It was reported in March 2000 that their leaders killed 924 members of the reclusive sect.

Response to Unfulfilled Predictions

All of these predictions failed; however, each of the movements precipitated by the predictions demonstrated the power of convictions to provoke life-changing commitments from people. Even more interesting was the human response in the face of unrealized expectations. According to Festinger, Riechen and Schacter, in a very detailed report of the human response to failed prophecies, they proved that even in the face of disconfirmation and the introduction of contrary evidence, there can still be an increase in the conviction and enthusiasm of the believers.[27] After the failure of

the prophecies, the members of the prophecy group seek to confirm their faith in the
group's teachings by attempting to "prose-
lyte" others and thereby reaffirming their
own inner belief system.[28] Melton J. Gordon presented a critique of Festinger in
which he argues that the predictions of
failed prophecies are not central to millen-
nialism since a well-organized group will
have many different topics on its agenda of
beliefs.[29] When prophecy fails, the group
tends to "spiritualize its predictions and
blame the failure on misunderstanding, not
error, in order to maintain the legitimacy of
the group and to reaffirm some accuracy to
the prophecy.[30] If the group has provided
for the possibility of failures, setbacks, opposition, and apostasy it has a mechanism of
resistance. A very common technique is the
establishment of a system of dualism or a
supernatural opponent that seeks to hinder
the movement. When the movement en-

counters resistance or the prophecies experience disconformation, it means that Satanic powers are at work because the victory of the movement is at hand. Therefore, failure of the prophecy is really a victory because it demonstrates the reality that the opposition is really in danger. These religious innovations apparently contribute, in part, to the survival of such groups in the face of failed prophecies.

Perhaps these references should prepare us for the possibility of a very long period during which the Gospel will continue to be the power of God and to seek to establish Christ's dominion over every area of human life. Our intellect should now recognize that all previous attempts to forecast the future in such a way have been discredited and to admit the fact that human history will continue for many thousands of years. Our interpretation of history should not be fatalistic. It has been the heritage of Biblical prophecy that has brought hope to a dying world. Our consciousness of the power of God and the evidence of His invading kingdom should free us from the paralyzing effect of a belief in inevitable destruction. God has acted in history and has a purpose for the world, a purpose being fulfilled through Christ and His Church. To reject the inevitable determinism of any belief in a decline in the activity of God in and through the Church will produce convictions and beliefs that are presented in the Scriptures.

The Basis of a Belief System

The foundations of most Christian belief systems rest upon basic concepts of the ultimate intentions and purposes of God. Advent teaching has frequently focused attention upon the imminence of the end of the world and this has hindered any hope of the Gospel's triumph. If we dismiss the doctrines of the end-times predictions and allow for a possibility of a long future for the earth, how will this affect our Christian activity? There are elements in the teaching of Jesus, which encourage hope for the continuing influence of the Gospel in the world. The Lord's Prayer testifies of the coming of

God's Kingdom with the phrase: "Thy will be done in earth as it is in heaven." The Lord's words before the High Priest take us back to Daniel's description of the Son of Man coming into God's presence and receiving "dominion, and glory, and a kingdom, that all the peoples, nations, and languages should serve him; his dominion is an everlasting dominion, which shall not pass away, and his kingdom that which shall not be destroyed" (7:14). Promises such as the "meek shall inherit the earth" (Matt. 5:5) are all admissions that Jesus expected a different concept of the future than has often dominated the attitude of the Church.

Judaism perhaps influenced the early belief system of Paul but later it advanced. In his earlier epistles, as mentioned before, Paul looked forward to a great apostasy, and the revelation of the man of sin as the immediate precursor of the Second Coming. Thus the history of the world was to

end with the culmination of evil and the
condemnation of the mass of humankind.
In Roman 11, the Apostle declares a progressive transformation of humanity
through the Gospel, culminating in the
conversion of the entire Gentile and Jewish
worlds as the prelude to the Second Coming.

The Jews believed that the divine intervention they expected would be preceded by a time of widespread apostasy and
the revelation of the Antichrist. The book
of Daniel gives some evidence of such beliefs. The figure described in Daniel represents Antiochus Epiphanes, the great per-
secutor of the Jews in the second century
B.C. The people were encouraged to re-
main faithful in their trials, recognizing
that all of these events had been foretold
and that the destruction of their enemies
would be followed by the triumph of God's
Kingdom. When Antiochus perished, no

golden age followed. The prophecy was viewed as being partially fulfilled and the man of sin was still to come in the future. Antiochus was simply a foreshadowing of the real Antichrist.

This belief passed into Christianity and can be seen in II Thessalonians 2, where the very words of Daniel reappear. Christians came to expect that the present age would reach its climax in a great apostasy and the appearance of the Antichrist. Such a belief system made it very difficult to envision the successful individual and cosmic work of the Gospel. If the Advent is to be expected soon and it is to be preceded by a reduction in the Church, there is little room for hope in Christian work.

The "falling away" is associated with the man of sin in 2 Thessalonians 2:3. Other related passages include 1 Timothy 4:1, 2 Timothy 3:1, and 2 Peter 3:2. But it must be understood that the writers speak of a development, which was already working among them. Paul speaks of the mystery of iniquity already at work (2 Thes. 2:7) and John also recognizes the existence of such antichristian activities when he declares:

> *"Little children, it is the last time: and as ye have heard that antichrist shall come, even now are there many antichrists; whereby we know that it is the last time. They went out from us, but they were not of us; for if they had been of us, they would have continued with us… Who is the liar but he that denieth that Jesus is the Christ? This is the antichrist, even he that denieth the Father and the Son" (1 John 2:18-22).*

The ideas of Antichrist and apostasy did not originate with the Christians but find their source in Jewish literature that expressed the mood of the apocalypses and their despair of the present.[31] Suffice to say that such expectation can have a depressing effect upon Christian endeavor where there persists a belief that the age must inevitably end in widespread apostasy.

Another basis for some belief systems is that a definite number of human souls is needed and as soon as this number is reached the end will come. In the *Book of Common Prayer* the burial service refers to the "number of thine elect" in the prayer which follows the committal and the Lord's Prayer: "Almighty God, with whom do live the spirits of them that depart hence in the Lord...beseeching thee, that it may please thee, of thy gracious goodness, shortly to accomplish the number of thine elect, and to hasten thy kingdom." These words seem to preclude any hope of final triumph of the Gospel and request the speedy culmination of human affairs. Such a belief that the age would end when a certain number of the elect had been reached would greatly influence evangelistic endeavors and focus attention upon individual salvation and gender a neglect of the cosmic claims of the Gospel.

The belief that the earth shall be filled with the glory of the knowledge of the Lord finds its origin in Isaiah 11:9. It has companion scriptures of hope to be found in Psalm 72; Isaiah 2:2-5, 9:2-7; 11:1-10, 32:15-17,40:4-11,42:1-12,49:1-26,56:3-8, 60:1-22, 61:1-11, 62:1-12, 65:1-25, 66:1-23; Psalm 2:6-8, Matthew 13:33, John 12:32 and others. Paul's word in Romans 11 shows that the time is coming when the whole world of mankind shall be brought into the subjection of Christ; the whole lump, all of the Jewish nation, and all the Gentiles in the world. John Wesley and John Newton had a conception of the victorious spread of the Gospel that was provoked by the hope elicited by these and other scriptures.[32] Such a hope played a significant part in the modern missionary movement.[33] Christopher Columbus filled his journals with quotations from Isaiah and other Biblical writers, in which he detailed the numerous prophecies that the Great Commission to disciple all nations of the world would be successful.[34]

It remains to be seen how a proper understanding of the purposes, intentions, and the overall rule of God as interpreted from the Scriptures can greatly influence the future expectations of a contemporary belief system. The late Archbishop Earl Paulk once made a very comprehensive statement that encompasses the reality of the kingdom of God:

> *"God's original purpose in creation was to establish and maintain a universal community in which there is creativity and productivity in an environment of health, peace and harmony.*

God's universe was corrupted by the chaos of rebellion and sin from both the angelic and the human worlds. Out of God's foreknowledge of these tragic insurrections, He decreed to ultimately destroy the curse of evil and restore all things back to the order and control of His eternal Kingdom and to the glory of His righteous rule. God has chosen to use redeemed humanity to correct the chaos of rebellion caused by the devil and to ultimately restore order and design to His universe. The Bible is the revelation of this divine activity of creation, redemption and the ultimate triumph of the will and purpose of God".[35]

The understanding of the above proposition is pivotal in any discussion of predictive prophecy regarding the church and the world. If the overall mission and eternal purpose to correct rebellion and to restore order and design to the universe under the ultimate rule of God is not fully understood as a divine and human priority, then our future perspective will be narrowed by the expectation of a literal destruction and defeat.

Influence of the Kingdom Concept

The reality of the kingdom of God is a subject of New Testament research that has provoked much controversy and evoked many diverse opinions. All factions generated by the controversy agree on the existence of the Kingdom of God but differ in their understanding of its nature, present implication and time of its appearance. It is viewed as being either a future hope, present spiritual blessings, a utopian existence or some socio-politically transformed state of being.

The mystery of the kingdom of God is that it involves a lot of things not fully understood. The fact that the principles and concepts of the kingdom of God can be at work in the midst of "tares" and all orga nized resistance is still a mystery. There are plural meanings of the kingdom that breed confusion to the natural mind when efforts are made to circumscribe it into a singular concept. For example, the kingdom is divine action, but it also involves human participation (Psalm 22:28; Matt. 6:10; 6:33); it is in some dimension now, but it is also past and future (Matt. 3:2; Mark 1:15; Psalm 145:13; Luke 10:9; Matt. 6:10); it is spiritual and it is physical (Luke 17:21; Jn. 18:36; Rom. 14:17; I Cor. 4:20); it is heavenly and it is also earthly (Luke 11:2; Rev. 5:10); and it is not of this world but operates within this world (John 18:36; Rev. 11:15). Howard Synder uses a system of models to explain the various polarities of the kingdom:

1. The kingdom as future hope; the future kingdom.
2. The kingdom as inner spiritual experience; the interior kingdom.
3. The kingdom as mystical communion; the heavenly kingdom.
4. The kingdom as institutional church; the ecclesiastical kingdom.
5. The kingdom as counter-system; the subversive kingdom.
6. The kingdom as political state; the theocratic kingdom.
7. The kingdom as Christianized culture; the transforming kingdom.
8. The kingdom as earthly Utopia; the Utopian kingdom.[36]

Such an expression of the multiple dimensions of the kingdom of God can be most helpful in understanding the human response factor, the temporal aspects (government, economics, laws, commerce etc.)

of the Kingdom and how God is involved in human affairs. If these polarities can be reconciled as being complementary rather than contradictory, perhaps a greater level of cooperative activity can occur among the different schools of thought concerning the Kingdom.

The Old Testament references to the kingdom of God are too numerous to dismiss it as simply a future existence (1 Chr. 29:11-13; Psalm 10:15, 103:19, 145:11-13; Isaiah 37:16). The opening of the New Testament begins with the message of John the Baptist: "Repent, for the Kingdom is at hand." Jesus preached about the kingdom of God and trained His disciples to carry out this same message (Matt. 3:1-2,4:17,23, 6:33, 9:35,24:14; Mark 1:14,15,4:11, 9:47, 10:14-25; Luke 4:23, 6:20, 9:11, 11:20, 12:31, 16:16, 17:20-21, 18:16-29; John 3:3,5; 18:36). The book of Acts is filled with the post-resurrection message of Jesus

– preaching about the kingdom of God (Acts 1:2-3, 8:8:12, 20:25-27, 28: 30-31).

The burden of apostolic preaching, as recorded in Acts, does not rest upon the expectation of the Second Coming of Christ.[37] It is only in Acts 3:20-21, that this expectation is explicitly presented, and only in Acts 10:42 that Christ is described as judge of the "quick and dead." It is implied in the whole of the preaching that Christ will come again! However, the point to be made is that the burden of apostolic preaching is that the unprecedented has happened, God has visited and redeemed His people, and the new creation has already been initiated through Christ.

The kingdom of God is the sovereign reign of God. The concept of the kingdom of God, which involves law, legislation and government, speaks of the priority, sovereignty, ability and right to act. The kingdom is the manifest priority of divine rule, and since all authority comes from God, any presumed authority that is in violation of divine rule is ultimately manifested in disorientation and disorganization. This is the state of fallen humanity, the world's system, which seeks to govern itself apart from and in contradiction to divine authority. It must be remembered that humanity was not created to rule apart from God. Mankind's original breach of covenant and efforts to rule without God introduced sin and confusion into the created order. Redemption is the restoration of divine order. The crisis of human misunderstanding of the kingdom of God rests in the comprehension or the lack of comprehension of the strategies of this transformation. That is one of the reasons why the earthly implications of the kingdom of God are often viewed from at least two extreme positions which range from a literal annihilation of the entire planet to the influential activities of the Holy Spirit working through an in-spired and theologically informed re-deemed community.

A further understanding of the king-dom of God is to be found in its redemp-tive and providential aspects.[38] The re-demptive kingdom involves all people, sys-tems, and structures that have willingly sub- mitted to the rule of God. The provi-dential kingdom involves the expressed sovereignty of God over all people, sys-tems, organizations, rule, government, an-imate and inanimate existence. In other words, the providence of God is expressed in His superintending power over all crea-tion. The redemptive kingdom is individu-al and "salvific" while the providential kingdom is corporate and cosmic. This differentiation is important since it liber-ates, in our minds, the belief that the Holy Spirit is not limited to the Church. Such a concept enables us to remove the barrier between the sacred and secular and provides for divinely inspired influential activity in every aspect of our lives.

Views of the Holy Spirit

The Kingdom is inseparable from the Holy Spirit (Rom. 14:17). The Holy Spirit is the dynamic of God's government. He is the executive agent of the Godhead and the mediator of all divine purposes and strategies. Pentecostal theology has erroneously declared that you receive the Holy Spirit in order to get to heaven; Roman Catholicism attempted to circumscribe the Holy Spirit to the sacraments, rituals, ordinances, and the ecclesiastical ministry; and the Evangelical community has regarded the Holy Spirit equally and not distinct from atonement, justification by faith, and Biblical doctrine. So we have been faced with these diverse views of the Holy Spirit ranging from an earthly experience with heavenly implications to an intellectual concept imprisoned within the sacraments, doctrines, creeds and ecclesiastical offices of the church. While in reality, the Holy Spirit has been active in all of these affairs while not being limited to the church. The Holy Spirit is actively involved in the government of the entire created order. It is important to realize the role of the Holy Spirit in history and in our contemporary world as He works to realign all things according to the will of God whether they be sacred, secular, civil, religious, earthly, heavenly, spiritual or natural.

Understanding Spiritual Language

The language of the Holy Spirit as recorded in historical proclamations and decrees has at times been misunderstood. Uncertainty over the literal and symbolical meaning of a historical text is the crisis of the interpretation process. The interpretation of typology, parables and prophecy has long been an issue of controversy. The fact that God has spoken in Holy Scripture is the very heart of our faith. God has spoken; but what has He said? This brings to our awareness the need of a system of hermeneutics. The primary function of a system of hermeneutics is to ascertain the meaning of the Word of God.

It is not in the scope of this discussion to deal with the various schools of interpretations, whether they be allegorical, literal, or liberal. However, may we focus on the controversy that arises when there is an improper tension between the literal and the symbolical meaning of a few historical texts. For example, the prophetic declaration of judgment to come upon several wicked nations is most interesting:

> *"Behold, the Day of the Lord is coming, cruel, with fury and burning anger, to make the land a desolation; and He will exterminate its sinners from it. For the stars of heaven and their constellations will not flash forth with their light; The sun will be dark when it rises, and the moon will not shed its light." (Isaiah 13:9-10) "And all the host of heaven will wear away, and the sky will be rolled up like a scroll; all their hosts will also wither away*

as a leaf withers from the vine, or as one withers from the fig tree." (Isaiah 34:4)

"And it will come about in that day, declares the Lord God, that I shall make the sun go down at noon and make the earth dark in broad daylight." (Amos 8:9)

Please note that none of these events literally took place. That is, the stars, moon, sun and the heavenly host were not literally disrupted. But the poetical and figurative language did describe the literal judgment of these wicked nations. Their leaders and rulers (stars, sun and moon) ceased to shine in power and the light of divine favor was "extinguished" over those nations.

The prophets perceived the *Day of the Lord* to be fulfilled in all of God's redemptive judgments in history against disobedient nations: it was the time of divine retri-

bution when the wicked would be annihi-
lated and the righteous saved and
blessed.[39] But the phrase, the *Day of the
Lord,* is also used in connection with the
first coming of the Lord. Malachi declared
that "Behold, I am going to send you Eli-
jah the prophet before the coming of the
great and terrible Day of the Lord" (Mai.
4:5-6). The Lord Jesus declared that this
prophecy was fulfilled in the ministry of
John the Baptist. The Day of the Lord
must be taken to mean many different
events and therefore its precise meaning
depends on the context. It always carries
the general idea of God coming in judgment and salvation.[40] However, it is not
simply associated with the destruction and
the annihilation of the entire created order.

Salvation is a comprehensive word. It
speaks of *re-creation* and *de-creation.* When
John refers to a "a new heaven and a new
earth, for the first heaven and the first

earth passed away," was he referring to the annihilation of the terrestrial and the celestial systems (Rev. 21:1)? Peter uses the same "collapsing-universe" terminology in describing "the present heavens and earth" (2 Peter 3:7). John Owen, a seventeenth-century Puritan theologian, described the Biblical usage of the terms "heavens and earth," as relating to Isaiah's vivid description of the Mosaic Covenant: "But I am the Lord thy God, that divided the sea, whose waves roared: The Lord of hosts is his name. And I have put my words in thy mouth, and I have covered thee in the shadow of mine hand, that I may plant the heavens, and lay the foundations of the earth, and say unto Zion, Thou art my people" (Isaiah 51:15-16). It was Owen's belief that whenever mention is made of the destruction of a state and government, it is in that language that seems to set forth the end of the world. And so the same "collapsing-universe" language is used in Isaiah 34:4 (the destruction of Edom), in Revelation 6:14 (the Roman Empire) and in Matthew 24 in which Jesus predicts the destruction of Jerusalem.[41]

The use of de-creation and re-creation phraseology involving the removing of the old earth and heavens, and the creation of a new earth and heaven refers, at times, to the period of the close of one dispensation, and the beginning of another.[42] The Old Covenant order and the central sanctuary of the Jerusalem Temple could be described as the "present heavens and earth." And the establishment of the Christian order would be spoken of in terms of removing the old earth and heavens, and the creation of a new earth and heavens.[43]

Throughout the New Testament, there is the use of the word "elements" in connection with the Old Covenant order. The writer of Hebrews rebuked the people for their need to be taught the "elements" of the oracles of God (Heb. 5:12). Paul corrected the Galatians for their preference of the "beggarly elements" of the Old Covenant legalism above the freedom of the New Covenant (Gal. 4:9). The epistle to the Colossians likewise uses the term "elements" to make a distinction between the Old Covenant rituals and ceremonies and freedom that are in Christ (Col. 2:8,20-21).

In all of the references to "elements" in Galatians, Colossians and Hebrews, the association is not with the physical world or universe but with the foundations of a religious system that was intended to pass away. The reference to the Old Covenant system and the approaching destruction of the Old Covenant Temple in A.D. 70 is the intended meaning of "elements."

The prophet Isaiah predicted the coming of "new things," longevity of human life, productivity, peace, and a time when people would build, plant, work and have children (Isaiah 65:17-25). The prophet foresaw an age, before the annihilation of the world, in which the gospel would accomplish its goal in transforming the earth and bringing to pass the goals of the kingdom of God. God had promised to bring a "new heaven and earth" by the work of Christ. The "new creation" spoken of by Isaiah could not be an eternal state, since it contains times of birth, death, building and planting (Isaiah 65:20-23). The passage represents the use of a symbolic phrase to describe the transformation of this present existence and a change in the way business would be done on this planet. Such phrases as the "the end of all things" (1 Peter 4:7) and "the end of the world" (Matt. 24:3, 6, 14, 34; Rom. 13:11-12) could only describe the dissolution of the Jewish temple based economy. The new contradiction to the old order of business that previously existed can best be described as simply being like a "new heaven and earth" in which there would dwell righteousness.

The apostles understood the Great Commission to the Church to be cosmic. The discipling of nations meant the subordination of families, individuals, commerce, government, education, social welfare, art, law, science, entertainment, and every sphere of human activity to the kingdom of God. The apostle Paul put it quite succinctly when he wrote: "He must reign, until He has put all enemies under His feet" (1 Cor. 15:25). The apostles did not visualize us being saved out of our environment but the restoration of the earth according to divine government. The Biblical language of de-creation symbolized in the destruction of the universe is symbolic of God's judgment, which is corrective and remedial.

Conclusion

Now what is the meaning of all these explanations? Well, it is simply to show that our interpretation of scriptural languages, especially prophecies, concerning the nature, the time and implications of the kingdom of God will greatly influence our perspective of the future. It presents the proposition that we can "prophesy" out of our doctrines or predict the outcome of future events according to our theological belief systems. If Christian victory is interpreted as an escape program rather than influential stewardship, then prophecies and predictions of future annihilation are plausible. If a "new heaven" and a "new earth" is a literal replacement of terrestrial and celestial structures rather than a transformation of the way business is done on this planet, then cosmic destruction is reasonable. If redemption is viewed predominantly as being the translation of the individual believers from earth to heaven rather than the reconciliation of the estranged planet community unto God, then perhaps the prophetic declarations of the end of all things could be at hand. But if the stewardship of the earth is a realized eschatology and the Gospel is the power of God unto salvation for the individual and the cosmos, then the future seems bright, though challenged, with opportunities for reformation.

There must, of necessity, be some conclusions drawn concerning the kingdom of God and how it relates to prophecies concerning the culmination of the ages. The kingdom of God is the priority of God and it concerns the way Christians live their daily lives. Therefore, the following are presented as propositions:

1. God rules over all times, seasons, as the Organizer and Maintainer of all things.

2. The movement of history toward ultimate triumph of divine purposes has been a pattern of death and resurrection, reformation and renewal. It has not been a pattern of annihilation.

3. The promise of the kingdom of God is a new social order where the individual and the environment are both reconciled to God's divine purposes. A new heaven and earth is concerned with the reconciliation of every sphere of human existence under the Lordship of Jesus Christ. But Jesus Christ is the "eschaton" and the

ultimate reconciliation of all things will not occur without Him.

4. The multiple polarities of the kingdom of God means it cannot be circumscribed into one singular concept. It exists separately and distinctly from the church and therefore has neither inherent weaknesses nor imperfections. The struggles of the church are not the struggles of the kingdom of God. However, the purposes of the kingdom of God are being projected into the church. The church is the embassy of the kingdom of God.

5. The kingdom of God comes by the working of the Holy Spirit with and through a redeemed community of Biblically informed, committed and obedient believers. It is the expression of the sovereignty of

God which also requires a human response.

6. Signs of the kingdom of God cannot be identified with wars, rumors of wars, earthquakes, floods, pestilence, plagues or any other kinds of disasters. The signs of the kingdom of God are the expressed manifestations of the consequences of the proclamations of the Gospel and the obedient responses of all creation

7. Predictive prophecies concerning the future must be reconciled to a Biblical understanding of the kingdom of God and the meaning of ultimate triumph of divine purposes.

8. The *language of* "de-creation" and "re-creation" speaks of the ethics of religious systems and not the physics of the universe. The radi-

cal changes in the foundational elements of religious systems are depicted in symbolical language.

The essence of Christianity is not to make predictions about the future but to perform the historical commandments of the Lord Jesus. Our task, as Christians, is to demonstrate the reality of the fact that He has come and the Lord has already visited His people. Predictions about "delays" and "comings" of the Lord are Biblically wrong. Our task is to evangelize and to demonstrate the principles of God in every area of human existence. And a preoccupation with the future at the expense of present day responsibilities of stewardship is the breeding ground for disappointment.

PART TWO
Personal

From the Eschatological to the Personal

What happens when prophecy is redirected from end-time issues to the personal welfare of the individual? What happens when individuals receive prophetic promises, decrees, and proclamations concerning their finances, relationships, possessions, occupations, and ministries and physical welfare? What is the human response to disconformations of personal prophecies? These are critical questions since Christians have been exposed to a tremendous amount of spiritual input through church pulpits, conferences, television ministries, books and tapes. Not only have they been exposed to external

input but many have become awakened to
the reality of the Holy Spirit and have experienced dreams, visions and revelations. All
of this charismatic activity has produced
various degrees of psychological and spiritual expectations among those who have
received such input.

It is important at the outset to place
personal prophecy in a proper perspective.
The theological and practical significance
of the Pauline epistles rest somewhat in
their tendency to place principles, concepts
and practices in proper relationship to one
another. Spiritual ministry, according to
Paul, should be decent, orderly, judged by
eldership, and a source of edification for
the whole Church (1 Cor. 12-14). It was
Paul who listed prophecy along with revelation, knowledge and doctrine as being
necessary ingredients for the profiting of
the saints (1 Cor. 14:6). Perhaps Paul's reference to prophecy may have included the

writings of the Old Testament prophets in addition to his personal ministry to the saints. Nevertheless, such a list places prophecy in a relationship with sound Biblical teaching and instruction. It also implies the responsibility of the believer to use common sense and sound judgment in making decisions affecting the issues of life. Scriptural prophecy is inspired speech that communicates divine purposes and intentions. It is profitable for encouragement, exhortation, comfort, reproof, rebuke, doctrine and instruction in righteousness. This is absolutely true when prophecy is directly aligned with divine purposes. Holy men of old spoke (prophesied) as the Holy Spirit moved upon them and their utterances and writings became the substance of the canonical Scriptures (Eph. 3:3-10; 2 Peter 1:19-21).

The prophecies and writings of all of the patriarchs were judged for their authenticity. Peter writes that no prophecy of the Scripture is based upon private interpretation and Paul demands that proper spiritual protocol requires all prophecies to be judged by the elders (2 Peter 1:20-21; 1 Cor. 14:29). There is the implication that spiritual ministry represents a mixture of the divine and human elements and must be judged for its content, intent and source.[44]

Let us bring our discussion into our contemporary setting. What happens when personal prophecies fail? Why do some spiritual predictions, warnings or insights prove to be erroneous? The answer rests in the source of the prophecies and the human response to the spiritual utterances. In 1982, Bishop Bill Hamon was introduced to Bishop Earl Paulk and the Chapel Hill Harvester Church leadership and staff. During a Tuesday night meeting, Bishop Hamon ministered prophetically to our entire presbytery and staff. The accuracy of his prophetic ministry was astonishing to all in attendance. The personal ministry addressed the ministry callings, giftings and provided valuable wisdom and insight that proved to be essential to the ongoing work of the ministry. Since that time, Bishop Hamon has provided strategic prophetic ministry and insight that has affected other areas of the Chapel Hill Harvester Church. The Christian International Ministry under Bishop Hamon has provided valuable conferences, seminars and resource materials to equip the Body of Christ in understanding the purpose, nature and governmental function of prophets and prophetic ministry.

Throughout the 1980's and 1990's, there has been an emphasis on the restoration of the office of the prophet and prophetic ministry, and a number of books have been written that have addressed some of the pitfalls of prophetic ministry.[45] As with every renewal emphasis, there were excesses and abuses and so it has been with this one. There have been allegations of the abuse of prophetic ministry to control and manipulate people and there have been evidences of false personal prophecies that have proven to be quite harmful. We have seen prophets who have lacked governmental understanding, and who have contributed to the disruption of local churches and ministries.

There is a tendency to correct abuse by censorship and disuse of a ministry; however, this is not always appropriate. Any of the five-fold ministry offices that function in an autonomous manner without due consideration of the governmental checks and balances of the other four will certainly produce extremes and errors. This is true of the pastors who have been guilty of heavy authoritarianism; it is true of teachers who have written and produced materials lacking true Biblical correctness; it is true of evangelists who have caused no small stir in local churches and conferences because of radical and erroneous "revelations"; it is true of apostles who have proposed the existence of a certain (apostolic) ecclesiastical hierarchy and who have claimed to have a higher level of revelation and governmental understanding; and it is certainly true of the bishops who have emerged with great fervor among Charismatic and Pentecostal groups and who have given the impression of a definite "elitism" of bishops. The corrections of all these extremes and abuses will not come effectively by censorship nor will it come through narrow Biblical scholarship that scandalizes the personality of ministry leaders. Forerunners of periods of renewals have traditionally suffered much criticism of their efforts and methods to restore a certain Biblical emphasis. They have had to suffer criticisms because of the "second generation" of ministers who did not totally adopt their principles and practices, and some of the criticisms may have been justified. However, the responsibility for the stewardship of a "move of God" does not rest solely in the hands of the forerunner. Such stewardship is a responsibility of the eldership of the corporate church and the more effective manner of discharging such stewardship responsibilities should be through meaningful dialogues and discussions among leaders.

The Psychology of False Prophecy

The Old Testament gives the clearest examples of prophetic ministry in the life of Israel. Prophets anointed and directed kings (1 Sam. 8-16); urged conformity to the law (Amos 4:1-13; Mic. 6:1-8); and set the stage for reformation and judgment (1 Sam.3:1-18; 1 Kings 13:1-10; 2 Chr. 16:7-9). Among the true prophets such as Jeremiah, Isaiah, Ezekiel, Samuel, Zechariah, Amos, and Micah, there were also false prophets. The prophets of Ahab and Jezebel (1 Kings 3:13); the unnamed groups mentioned by Jeremiah (Jer. 5:31; 14:14; 23:32; 29:9); and the false prophet Hananiah that Jeremiah

(Jer. 28) encountered represent just a few examples.

False prophecy was not so easily identified as a system or an institution opposed to true prophecy, but it came about by a gradual process of corruption.[46] The gradual deterioration of one originally gifted with the capacity for prophecy, the loss of moral fiber, the increasing loss of moral vision, the invasion of the conscience by a spirit of self-deception contributed to an inevitable degeneration of the office.[47] Self-deception, disobedience to God, desire for gain and popularity contributed to the delusion of the prophet and ultimately the delusion of the people. Because the false prophet resembled his more faithful brother or sister in the possession of the prophetic temperament, one can readily see how the false prophet could easily have influenced the people through words, visions and dreams. This was especially true of

Hananiah's prediction of a speedy return from the exile (Jer. 28).

Deception by the Lord

There is another dimension in which the Lord deceived the false prophet. The Lord used the false prophet as an instrument to effect punishment on the people for their disobedience. This is evident in the phrase, "And if the prophet be deceived and speaketh a word, I the Lord have deceived that prophet" (Ezek. 14:9). The incident of Micaiah and the prophets of Ahab further demonstrate the activity of divine authority in the deception of the prophet (2 Chr. 18:18-22).

It also demonstrates the fact that deceptive and false counsel is the divine sentence against sustained disobedience to the

Lord. The apostle Paul mentions the consequences of sustained disobedience to the
Lord in his epistle to the Thessalonians:
"And for this cause God shall send them
strong delusion, that they should believe a
lie; that they all might be damned who
believed not the truth, but had pleasure in
unrighteousness" (2 Thess. 2:11-12). Spiritual blindness and the inability to discern
is a manifestation of divine judgment
against ungodliness.

Teaching Rebellion

The identity of the false prophets and their ministries are best encapsulated in the following phrase, "Thou hath taught rebellion against the Lord" (Jer. 28:16; 29:32). Rebellion against the Lord can be generated by a misinterpretation of divine priorities and promises, which results in patterns of direct violations of decrees and statues. The account of such rebellion was demonstrated in the confrontation between Jeremiah and Hananiah (Jer. 28:1-17). Jeremiah predicted the judgment of Judah and the promise of restoration from exile. Jeremiah predicted the design and duration of the judgment. Hananiah who was Jeremiah's contemporary, prophesied a return of the captives after two years of captivity and encouraged the people to resist the captivity (Jer. 28:1-17). The judgment of the Lord against Hananiah was encapsulated in the words: "Therefore, thus saith the Lord, behold I will cast thee from off the face of the earth; this year thou shalt die, because thou has taught rebellion against the Lord" (Jer. 28:16).

A further identity of false prophetic ministry is demonstrated in its emphasis on lesser priorities and values. For example, prophetic teachings that misdirect the ministry goals of the church away from its present stewardship of the earth and causes the church to become apathetic and preoccupied with the future is the teaching of rebellion. Personal spiritual input that places an unreasonable focus upon personal wealth and possessions deludes the hearer and sets him/her on a course that ultimately leads them away from true service to the Lord. It was Jesus who admonished the people for their preoccupation with earthly possessions and their lack of concern for the kingdom of God (Luke 12:22-31). It is quite clear that spiritual input can direct the priorities, values, goals, aspirations, attitudes, and activities of the hearers. So rebellion becomes an issue of inappropriate priorities, goals, and aspirations.

It is becoming clear that it is difficult to separate the discernment of the prophet or prophecies from the content and intent of the messages. It is not so much that the spiritual message denies the Lord or even confesses that Jesus is Lord that determines its character (1 John 4:1-3; 1 Cor. 12:3). It is when the ultimate intent of the spiritual input is to ensnare the believers or to turn them away from the true priorities, values, and responsibilities of being a Christian that it becomes false (Acts 13:6-10). For example, the wealth of the sinner is laid up for the just (Prov. 13:22) is but a preoccupation with the gaining of personal wealth and riches at the expense of other stewardship responsibilities and becomes a diversion.

Prophetic Talk

Misinterpretation is another issue. The meanings of prophecies are most often revealed in the terminology, symbolism and literalism of the messages. Bishop Hamon gives an interesting observation concerning the terminology of personal prophecies:

> ***Immediately*** means from one day to three years.
>
> ***Very soon*** means one to ten years.
>
> ***Now*** or ***this day*** means one to forty years.
>
> ***I will*** without a definite time designation means God will act sometimes in the person's life if he/she is obedient.

Soon was the term Jesus used to describe the time of His soon return almost two thousand years ago.[48]

Such terminology seems to indicate that all prophetic promises or decrees are conditional, and they involve a process – whether it is stated or not (Jer. 18:8-10; Ezek. 18:21-24). The promise that David would be king took years of adversity before being realized. The promise of prosperity may involve work, commitment, and perseverance. The promise of healing may involve medical intervention. The promise of deliverance may include the presence of continued negative circumstances. The promise of victory may include a series of setbacks. In essence, the process should not be interpreted as the confirmation or disconfrrmation of the genuine promise.

Demand for the Supernatural

There are times when promises fail because there is a demand for a supernatural event to occur when a natural event will accomplish God's goal. The disruptions of neither the natural courses of life nor the intervention of some unusual series of events are not the only ways of prophetic fulfillment. Naaman, the captain of the host of the king of Syria, was about to forfeit a prophetic promise for healing because he thought that the cleansing of his leprosy should come through some spectacular demonstration by Elisha rather than following the instructions of the prophet to dip seven times in the Jordan (2 Kings 5). Many prophetic promises fail because of the reluctance of the recipient to cooperate and perform natural tasks.

Deadly Delays

There are times that prophecies fail simply because of procrastination. According to the *American College Dictionary,* to procrastinate means "to defer an action; to put off till another day or time." Hence, when you delay or put something off you are procrastinating, regardless of the reason for the delay. Simply speaking, procrastination is the behavior of postponing. The roots of procrastination lie in fear and ignorance. Generally, there is a fear of failure or a fear of losing something or someone and so, there is a delayed response out of fear of being separated from whatever is familiar or needed. Ignorance of how to respond properly is another factor. When all of the facts and information are not available, then it is conceivable that there will be a delayed response to a directive; however, much procrastination occurs not because of lack of knowledge but because of fear of the consequences. So, we use such terminology as "waiting on the Lord" or "waiting for the right timing" when all of the necessary information is available. There are many other legitimate and illegitimate reasons for "putting off until tomorrow what should be done today," but procrastination is a major cause of failed prophecies.

Misunderstanding His Ways

The ways of the Lord are a source of intrigue when dealing with this subject, for His ways are quite different from ours (Isaiah 55:8). For example, He chooses two senior citizens, Abraham and Sarah, to bring forth a promised child; He sends a servant, Joseph, into captivity at the hands of his brothers in order to preserve the future of Israel; He promises deliverance of Israel by sending them into Babylonian captivity; He instructs a servant, Hezekiah, to use a mixture of figs for healing; and He uses the weak things to confound the mighty things.

Many years ago, the Lord promised that He would give visibility to our local church, and we expected newspaper journalists, magazine writers, and television stations to converge upon the church and record the wonderful ministry. Instead, a very disruptive series of events occurred that attracted the attention of the media and suddenly the Chapel Hill Harvester Church was a national and international news item. Toward the end of the crisis, I was impressed with the thought, "I told you that I would give this church visibility!" Well, I certainly did not think it would come through a series of negative events that commanded a worldwide audience!

Missing the Meaning

It is unfortunate that many prophecies and promises fail because of the misinterpretation of the scope of the content. For example, Abraham received a promise from the Lord that nations of the earth would be blessed through him (Gen. 12:2; 17:5-9) and a promise for the generations of his descendants. Here is a principle that is often missed and it becomes a source of disappointment. A promise can be given to an individual, who is a representative of a greater cause, and the individual can reduce the corporate scope of the promise to a personal one. I recall an associate minister of a large church who presented a tape of a personal prophecy he had received and as I listened to the recording, it became obvious to me that the message was given to this individual as a representative of that local church. The message involved a promise of growth, geographic relocation, and financial provisions; however, the minister was about to take the message as a confirmation that it was time for him to separate himself from the local church and began a new work. It is important that the individual and corporate meaning of spiritual input be understood.

Personal Desires

There are experiential aspects of Christianity that are very subjective and not always measurable. For example, personal dreams, visions, revelations and impressions are subjective experiences that are difficult to integrate into our daily routines. How do you interpret and apply such subjective experiences to the daily decision making process? Even though the Scriptures are filled with examples of counsel and direction being given through such channels of guidance, there are problems often encountered with such personal spiritual input. The problem is compounded when such spiritual input involves matters of emotional attachments such as relationships, finances, occupations, health, sickness, geographic relocations and so forth. We are rational and emotional creatures with the ability to express strong desires and needs, and there are times when personal desires and ambitions are mistaken for true spiritual input. A pastor related to me the following story concerning the purchase of a property. He had been in an extended building program that had been financially and emotionally taxing upon him and the local congregation and he was anxious to bring closure to the project. Within a few months short of retiring the debt of the new construction, a property was made available to the church; but the strong emotional attachment that he and the local elders had to the closure of the current debt caused them to believe that they had been "impressed of the Lord" not to venture into any new purchase. However, for months after the decision, the pastor was restless in his spirit. When a friend asked him about the property and encouraged him to reconsider the purchase, he contacted the new owners of the property. Fortunately, the new owners had undergone some re-organization and needed to sell the property, so it was purchased and converted into a much-needed facility for the youth. This represents an example where an emotional attachment to the closure of a debt and the unwillingness to engage a new burden was the motivation behind an "inner witness" or a "personal impression" that was interpreted as true spiritual directions.

Good Doubt

We should be suspicious about all personal impressions or "hunches" that involve matters of personal emotional attachment. We should also learn to think ahead before making decisions supported only by personal subjective input such as an "inner witness." When there is a strong desire for anything, there is the possibility that anything that is heard or seen can become a confirmation. We can be suspicious of ourselves without being skeptical and shipwrecked in our faith. A young woman discussed with me a personal "inner witness" she had concerning the reconciliation of her estranged husband. She had been married for ten years when her husband abandoned her and their two small children, and after seven years of separation, he filed for a divorce. She felt impressed in "her spirit" that her husband would eventually have a "Saul of Tarsus experience on the Damascus road" and return to her. Thus, she lived in great expectation of such an event for years. Every sermon, exhortation and encouragement that was given by a minister during a church service, conference or even through television, she interpreted as a confirmation of her inner impression. When the divorce became final and her ex-husband remarried and began a new family, she was shattered. She was upset with God, as well as the prophets and television evangelists. When we discussed her responsibility in the crisis, she was at first reluctant to accept any responsibility for her self-deception. However, when we explored such issues as emotional attachments, personal desires and the simple nature of being human, she gradually assumed responsibility without feeling condemned. We must remember that we are fallible human beings capable of imagination, projection, and fantasy. We are capable of a scale of emotions ranging from despair and depression to hope, joy, optimism, and faith. We are imperfect, so we are subject to making mistakes in judgment. However, there are tools such as knowledge of the Scriptures, the Holy Spirit, common sense, wise counsel, and even past experiences that can help us to manage our humanity.

Conclusion

What is the sum of all of this? There must be a perspective given here, and I think there are some principles to be observed:

1. Prophetic ministry is a revelation of purposes, intentions, and promises of God.
2. Prophetic ministry must be judged for its content and intent.
3. The human response to prophecy should be conditioned by the Scripture, counsel, common sense, and the lessons learned from past experiences.

4. To test against Scripture and to ask questions is not an expression of doubt or an indication of a lack of faith.

5. Impatience, misinterpretation and misapplication can distort spiritual input.

6. Procrastination is a vital cause of disobedience.

7. Emotional needs and desires can be misinterpreted as spiritual input.

8. Prophetic consensus is the presentation of the same Divine information in different places through different people.

9. Prophetic contradiction is the introduction of events and circumstances that create suspicion concerning the accuracy and source of the Divine information.

10. The mystery of prophecy is the idea that God declares the end from the beginning but often omits the middle part which the process of fulfillment.

When spiritual disappointment does occur there are several points to consider:

1. Remember that God is always faithful and intends the best for His people.
2. Human failures and weakness can be beneficial experiences.
3. Do not shipwreck your faith because of spiritual disappointment.
4. Forgive yourself and others, if spiritual input has been erroneous.
5. Do not close off your willingness and ability to receive future spiritual input.

There shall come a time of the ultimate fulfillment of all things and at the Coming of the Lord when prophecies shall fail, tongues shall cease and knowledge shall vanish away. Until that time, may we use prophecies, tongues, knowledge and discernment for His glory!

END NOTES

[1] J.I. Packer, *God Has Spoken* (Grand Rapids: Baker Books, 1979), p. 114.

[2] H. Richard Niebuhr, *The Social Sources of Denominationalism* (New York: Henry Holt and Company, 1929).

[3] A. Berkeley Mickelsen, *Interpreting The Bible* (Grand Rapids: Eerdmans, 1989), p. 212-218.

[4] William Barclay, *The King and The Kingdom* (Grand Rapids: Baker Book House, 1968), p. 109.

[5] Ibid.

[6] E.W. Rogers, *Concerning the Future* (Chicago: Moody Press, 1962), p.26.

[7] Gary DeMar, *Last Day Madness* (Atlanta, Georgia: American Vision, 1997).

[8] Marvin Rosenthal, *The Pre-Wrath Rapture of the Church* (Nashville, TN: Thomas Nelson, 1990).

[9] Henry Van Etten, *George Fox and the Quakers* (New York: Harper Torchbooks, 1959), p. 7

[10] Roland H. Bainton, *The Reformation of the Sixteenth Century* (Boston: Beacon Press, 1956), p. 24

[11] Coretta Scott King, *The Words of Martin Luther King, Jr.* (New York: Newmarket Press, 1967), p. 67

[12] C.H. Dodd, *The Coming of Christ* (Cambridge: University Press, 1951), p. 1-11.

[13] P. Hughes, *A Popular History of the Catholic Church* (New York: Doubleday and Company, 1954), p. 10.

[14] Ibid.

[15] Will Durant, *The Story of Civilization* (New York: Simon and Schuster, 1966), pp. 603-604.

[16] Ibid.

[17] T. Francis Glasson, *His Appearing and His Kingdom* (The Epworth Press: London, 1953), p. 46.

[18] Ibid.

[19] Richard Heath, *Anabaptism: From Its Rise at Zwickau to Its Fall at Munster, 1521-1536* (London: Alexander and Shepheard, 1895), p. 119. This is one of the *Baptist Manuals: Historical and Biographical,* edited by George P. Gould.

[20] Ibid.

[21] Francis D. Nichol, *The Midnight Cry* (Tacoma Park, Washington, D.C.: Review and Herald Printing Company, 1944).

[22] Nichols, p. 209-210.

[23] "Charles Taze Russell, *The Time is at Hand,* Watch-tower Bible and Tract Society, 1914), p. 99-100.

[24] Herbert W. Armstrong, 7975 *in Prophecy,* p. 10,12, quoted in The Watchman Expositor (Watchmen Fellowship, Inc., 1998). p. 2.

[25] Richard Abanes, *End-Time Visions* (New York: Broadman & Holman, 1998), p. 24.

[26] Craig Nelson, Cult Survivors: Kanungu, Uganda (Associated Press, April 3, 2000).

[27] Leon Festinger, Henry W. Riecken and Stanley Schaehter, *When Prophecy Fails* (Minneapolis. University of Minnesota Press, 1956).

[28] Ibid

[29] Gordon J. Melton, *"What Really Happens When Prophecy Fails.* An unpublished paper presented at The Conference on American

Millenruausm Um-ficadon Theological
Seminary, Banytown, N.Y.,1980.

30 Ibid

31 T. Francis Glasson, *His Appearing and His
Kingdom* (London: The Epworth Press,
1953), p. 118.

32 Lain H. Murray, *The Puritan Hope: A
Study in Revival and the Interpretation of Prophecy*
(Carlisle, Pennsylvania: The Banner of
Truth, 1971), p. 131-155.

33 Ibid

34 David Chilton, *Paradise Restored* (Reconstruction Press: Tyler, Texas, 1985), p. 6.

35 Earl Paulk and Daniel Rhodes, A *Theology the Next Millennium* (Decatur, Georgia:
Cathedral of the Holy Spirit, 1999).

36 Howard A. Synder, *Models of the Kingdom*
(Nashville: Abingdon Press, 1991).

37 C.H. Dodd, *The Apostolic Preaching and* its *Development* (London: Hodder and Stouchton Limited, 1951).

38 Era Baxter, *A Daring Biblical Approach to God's Agenda for the Church* (Shippensburg, Pa.: Destiny Image, 1995). This represents notes taken from lectures given by Ern Baxter at the Cathedral of the Holy Spirit from 1990 to *1995.*

39 David Chilton, *Paradise Restored: An Eschatology of Dominion* (Tyler, Texas: Reconstruction Press, 1985), p. 137.

40 Ibid., p. 138

41 John Owen, "Providential Changes, An Argument for Universal Holiness," *The Works of John Owen,* 16 vols. (London: Banner of Truth Trust, 1965-68), 9:134.

42 John Brown, *Discourse and Sayings of Our Lord,* 3 vols. (Edinburgh: The Banner of Truth Trust, 1990), 1:171-72.

43 Brown, *Discourse and Sayings,* 172.

44 Kirby and Sandra Clements, *Discernment* (Decatur, Georgia: Cathedral Press, 1999), p. 49-70.

45 Bishop Bill Hamon has authored several books which include: *Prophets, Pitfalls and Principles: God's Prophetic People Today* (Shippensburg, Pa.: Destiny Image, 1991), *Prophets and Personal Prophecy: God's Prophetic Voice Today* (Shippensburg, Pa.: Destiny Image, 1987), *Prophets and the Prophetic Movement: God's Prophetic Move Today* (Shippensburg, Pa.: Destiny Image, 1990) and *Apostles, Prophets and the Coming Moves of God: God's End-Time Plans for His Church and Planet Earth* (Shippensburg, Pa.: Destiny Image, 1997).

46 G.C. Joyce, *The Inspiration of Prophecy* (New York: Oxford University Press, 1910), p. 129-137.

[47] Ibid.

[48] Bill Hamon, *Prophets and Personal Prophecy: Guidelines for Receiving, Understanding, and Fulfilling God's Personal Word to You* (Shippensburg, Pa.: Destiny Image, 1987), p. 123.

ABOUT THE AUTHOR

For more than 20 years, Dr. Kirby Clements served as associate pastor to the late Archbishop Earl Paulk at the 12,000-member Cathedral of the Holy Spirit. In 1999, he was installed as Bishop of the Harvester Network of Churches worldwide.

Currently, he is founder of The Community of the Holy Spirit, a local church in Decatur, Georgia. He is also the founder and chief executive office of The International Connection of Ministries, an outreach organization that provides training and support to ministry organizations throughout Africa, Europe, South America, United States, and Caribbean. He also serves as the presiding leading of The International Communion of Charismatic Churches, a trans-denominational group of national and international leaders and ministries.

He travels extensively representing the office of the Archbishop, both nationally and internationally, and he has authored 12 books, along with his late wife, Pastor Sandra Clements.

CPSIA information can be obtained
at www.ICGtesting.com
Printed in the USA
BVHW072026011118
531619BV00001B/4/P